All About Wildebeests

Katie Gillespie

EYEDISCOVER

Go to **www.eyediscover.com** and enter this book's unique code.

BOOK CODE

R459572

EYEDISCOVER brings you optic readalongs that support active learning.

Published by AV² by Weigl
350 5th Avenue, 59th Floor New York, NY 10118
Website: www.eyediscover.com

Library of Congress Control Number: 2017930733

ISBN 978-1-4896-5710-7 (hardcover)

Printed in the United States of America
in Brainerd, Minnesota
1 2 3 4 5 6 7 8 9 0 21 20 19 18 17

022017
020317

Editor: Katie Gillespie
Designer: Mandy Christiansen

Weigl acknowledges Getty Images, iStock, Alamy, Shutterstock, and Dreamstime as the primary image suppliers for this title.

EYEDISCOVER provides enriched content, optimized for tablet use, that supplements and complements this book. EYEDISCOVER books strive to create inspired learning and engage young minds in a total learning experience.

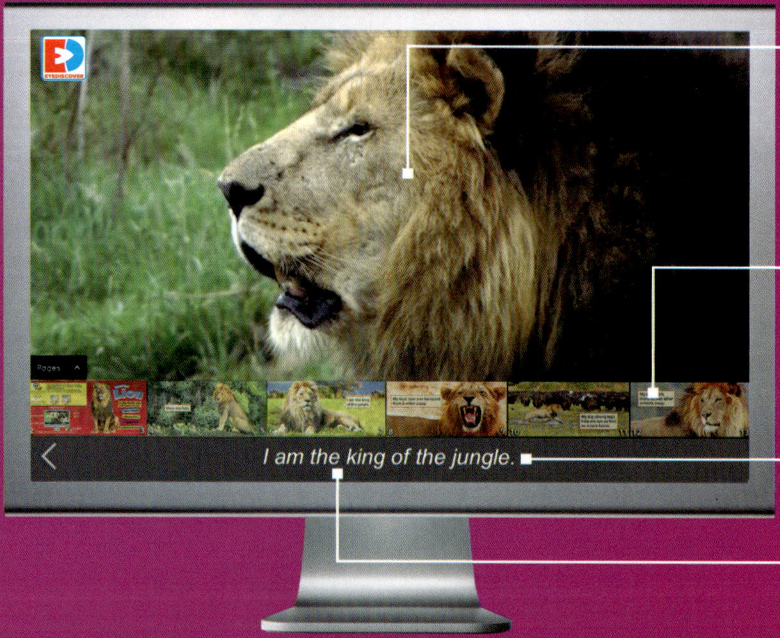

Watch
Video content brings each page to life.

Browse
Thumbnails make navigation simple.

Read
Follow along with text on the screen.

Listen
Hear each page read aloud.

Your EYEDISCOVER Optic Readalongs come alive with...

Audio
Listen to the entire book read aloud.

Video
High resolution videos turn each spread into an optic readalong.

OPTIMIZED FOR

- ✓ TABLETS
- ✓ WHITEBOARDS
- ✓ COMPUTERS
- ✓ AND MUCH MORE!

All About

Wildebeests

In this book, you will learn about

- how they look
- where they live
- what they eat

and much more!

Wildebeests are mammals with sharp horns. They are also known as gnus.

Wildebeests live in Africa. They make their homes on woodlands and grassy plains.

Baby wildebeests are called calves. They can walk only minutes after being born.

There are two kinds of wildebeests. They are different sizes and colors.

Wildebeests are part of a group called antelopes. Antelopes have hoofs and graze for food.

Wildebeests eat plants.
Their favorite food is grass.

Wildebeests live in large groups called herds. This helps keep them safe from danger.

About 1.5 million wildebeests move together every summer to find food and water.

It is important that wildebeests get enough to drink. They must be near water to stay happy and healthy.

WILDEBEESTS BY THE NUMBERS

Wildebeests can **weigh** up to **600 pounds.** (270 kilograms)

Male wildebeests leave their herd when they are 1 year old to **start a new group.**

A wildebeest's horns can be about **3 feet across.** (1 meter)

The **wildebeest migration** is **one** of the **seven wonders** of the **natural world.**

Wildebeests have **a life span** of

up to

years.

Up to **500,000 wildebeest calves** are born **each year.**

KEY WORDS

Research has shown that as much as 65 percent of all written material published in English is made up of 300 words. These 300 words cannot be taught using pictures or learned by sounding them out. They must be recognized by sight. This book contains 51 common sight words to help young readers improve their reading fluency and comprehension. This book also teaches young readers several important content words, such as proper nouns. These words are paired with pictures to aid in learning and improve understanding.

Page	Sight Words First Appearance
4	also, are, as, known, they, with
7	and, homes, in, live, make, on, their
8	after, being, can, only
11	different, kinds, of, there, two
12	a, food, for, group, have, part
15	eat, is, plants
16	from, helps, keep, large, them, this
19	every, find, move, to, together, water
20	be, enough, get, important, it, must, near, that

Page	Content Words First Appearance
4	gnus, horns, mammals, wildebeests
7	Africa, plains, woodlands
8	calves, minutes
11	colors, sizes
12	antelopes, hoofs
15	grass
16	danger, herds
19	summer

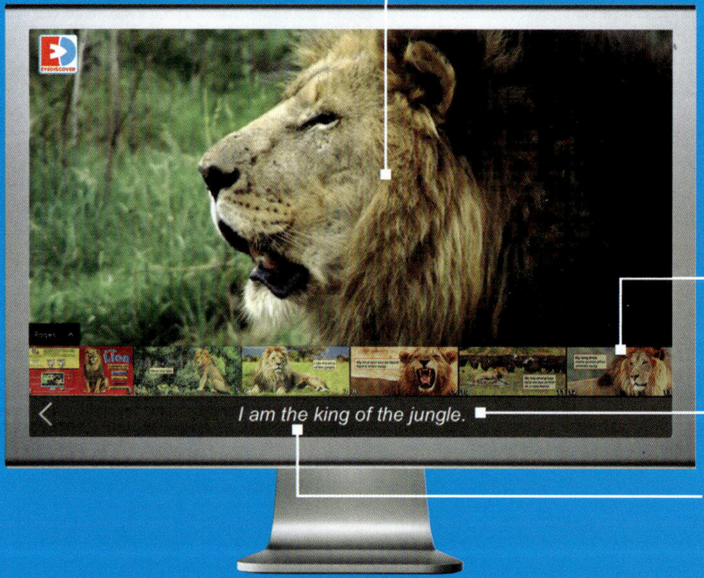

Watch
Video content brings each page to life.

Browse
Thumbnails make navigation simple.

Read
Follow along with text on the screen.

Listen
Hear each page read aloud.

EYEDISCOVER

Go to www.eyediscover.com and enter this book's unique code.

BOOK CODE

R459572